LET'S TALK ABOUT
BEING GOOD

by Joy Berry • Illustrated by Maggie Smith

Copyright© Joy Berry, 2022
Originally Published, 1995

All rights are reserved.

No part of this book can be duplicated or used without the prior written permission of the copyright owner, except for the use of brief quotations from the book.

For inquiries or permission requests contact the publisher.

Published by Joy Berry Enterprises
www.joyberryenterprises.com

Hello, my name is Iggy.

I live with Michael.

Most of the time Michael behaves in a good way.

Most of the time he thinks about other people's feelings.

Michael makes other people feel good when he is kind to them.

He makes others feel good when he shares his things.

But no one is perfect, and neither is Michael.

Sometimes he accidentally does something wrong.

Sometimes you might accidentally do something wrong, too.

Sometimes you might do something wrong on purpose.

Sometimes another person might tell you to do something wrong, and you might do it.

Sometimes another person might bother you so much that you do something you shouldn't, just to make him or her stop.

Sometimes another person might try to get you to do something wrong by threatening you.

It's very hard to be good all the time.

But you're responsible for your actions.

No matter what might happen, try to do the right thing.

Try to be careful so that you don't accidentally do things that are wrong.

Avoid playing roughly with others.

Be extra cautious around things that break easily.

Use things the way they're supposed to be used.

Try not to do things that are wrong on purpose.

Find out what the rules are and try to follow them.

Don't let people talk you into doing things that are wrong.

Tell them no, or walk away.

Try to stay away from people who bother you.

When this isn't possible, do your best to ignore them.

Or just walk away.

Walk away from anyone who threatens you.

If possible, get help from an adult.

Nobody is perfect.

Sometimes you might do something wrong.

When you do, admit it and say you're sorry.

Then do whatever you can to make the situation better.

It's best for everyone when you try your hardest to be good!

Let's talk about... **Joy Berry!**

As the inventor of self-help books for kids, Joy Berry has written over 250 books that teach children about taking responsibility for themselves and their actions. With sales of over 80 million copies, Joy's books have helped millions of parents and their kids.

Through interesting stories that kids can relate to, Joy Berry's Let's Talk About books explain how to handle even the toughest situations and emotions. Written in a clear, simple style and illustrated with bright, humorous pictures, the Let's Talk About books are fun, informative, and they really work!

www.ingramcontent.com/pod-product-compliance
Lightning Source LLC
Chambersburg PA
CBHW081411070526
44583CB00020B/2767